EASY TO PATCHWORK

EASY TO PATCHWORK

Lynette Mostaghimi

SERIES CONSULTANT: EVE HARLOW

BROCKHAMPTON PRESS
LONDON

First published in Great Britain in 1991
by Anaya Publishers Ltd, Strode House,
44-50 Osnaburgh Street, London NW1 3ND
Reprinted 1992, 1993

This edition published 1996 by Brockhampton Press,
a member of Hodder Headline PLC Group

Editor Eve Harlow
Designer Mike Leaman
Photography Di Lewis
Illustrator Kate Simunek
Artwork Julie Ward
Text editor Judith Casey

British Library Cataloguing in Publication Data

Mostaghimi, Lynette
Easy to patchwork. – (Easy to make)
1. Patchwork
I. Title II. Series
746.46
ISBN 1-86019-109-6

Typeset by Tradespools Limited, Frome, Somerset, UK
Colour Reproduction by Columbia Offset, Singapore
Printed and bound in EC

CONTENTS

Introduction

The craft of patchwork originates from times when cloth was scarce and expensive. It was a way of combining warmth and decoration with economy, and evolved into one of the finest folk arts.

The craft is reputed to have arrived in England with the 12th- and 13th-century Crusaders. However, it is probably much older. Archaeological evidence suggests that patchwork was used by earlier generations, some 3,000 years ago.

English patchwork developed along with appliqué and quilting, often combining all three skills in the same piece. Wool was probably the first fabric to be used but no examples survive. In the 18th century, colourful and hardwearing chintz cottons imported from India became the favourite fabrics for patchwork. It is from this date that the oldest quilt in England originates: the Levens quilt from Levens Hall, near Kendal, Cumbria in the north of England, was made in 1708. In the early 17th century, patchwork travelled to the New World with the pilgrims, where the craft flourished and developed into an art form.

Patchwork today

In both Europe and America, the tradition of patchwork continues to thrive and increase in popularity with successive generations. Most homes have a few remnants of fabric tucked away, too small to make any one garment but too beautiful to discard. Patchwork makes it possible to use every piece of fabric, no matter how small, and the final result can be wonderfully rewarding.

Equipment

Your sewing basket will contain almost all you need for patchwork. A pair of sharp, medium-sized scissors is essential. You will also need fine dressmaking pins, and fine 'sharps' sewing needles. It is also helpful if you train yourself to use a thimble.

Templates, geometric shapes made of metal or plastic, are used to cut fabrics and

backing papers accurately. These are widely available in crafts shops and on needlework and notions counters. However, you can make your own templates from stiff card. All the templates for the projects in this book are illustrated full size; some are on pages 8–11, others are on page 95. For accuracy use a pencil and ruler to draw the shapes, and cut cardboard with a sharp knife on a protected surface. Select good quality paper for the backing papers, but not shiny paper as this will slip.

Golden rules

The main points to successful patchwork are, above all, accuracy in cutting out the papers and then folding the fabric corners. Very neat, tiny oversewing stitches should be used to join the patches. Another secret is the balancing of colour and the proportion of the shapes. Because each piece is worked individually, you can 'play' with the arrangement to complement colours and textures before sewing patches together.

Adding special effects can also contribute to the beauty of patchwork. Search haberdashery counters for new ideas, such as sequins, bows and beads. Use them to complement your design, but be careful not to let them dominate your work.

Finally, enjoy the craft, follow your instinct for colour and harmony and the results will be stunning.

Choosing fabrics

Although patchwork is a craft with its roots in economy, modern patchworkers tend to buy new fabrics for a project, mixing and matching colours from the co-ordinated ranges available. However, this does not mean that you cannot have the fun of building your patchwork from your remnants bag. You just to have to be a little careful about the fabrics you use.

Whether you have saved pieces from dressmaking or bought remnants at sales (or even cut up outworn garments), always wash the fabric carefully to see if there is any colour-run and to make sure that the fabric is pre-shrunk. Discard any fabrics that are not colour-fast.

As far as possible, patchwork should be made of fabrics of similar weight so that there is no dragging or pulling of stitches. Semi-sheer fabrics should be mounted on lightweight cotton first. Generally, it is unwise to mix heavy or piled fabrics – such as velvet – with smooth types.

Patchwork templates

Here, and on pages 10–11, are the templates you need for most of the projects in this book. Trace them carefully, using a ruler, then transfer the shape to stiff card. Use the templates to cut papers from stiff notepaper. Add ¹/₄in (6mm) all round when cutting fabric.

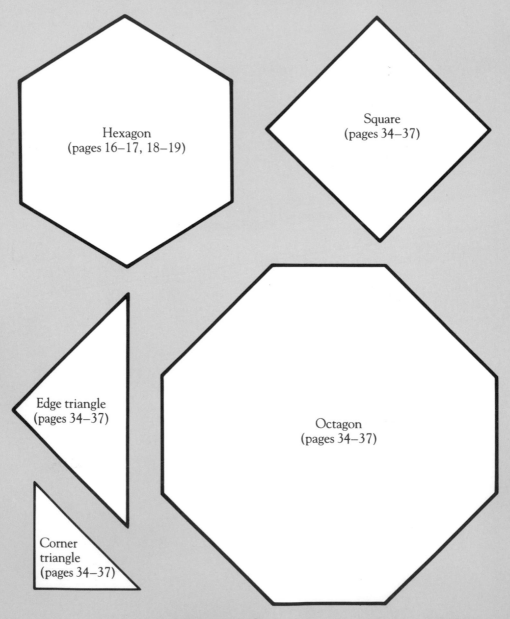

Hexagon
(pages 16–17, 18–19)

Square
(pages 34–37)

Edge triangle
(pages 34–37)

Octagon
(pages 34–37)

Corner
triangle
(pages 34–37)

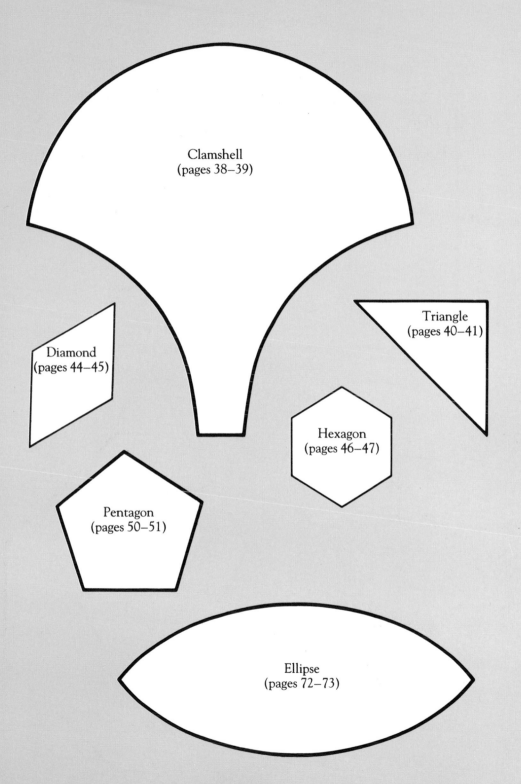

Clamshell
(pages 38–39)

Triangle
(pages 40–41)

Diamond
(pages 44–45)

Hexagon
(pages 46–47)

Pentagon
(pages 50–51)

Ellipse
(pages 72–73)

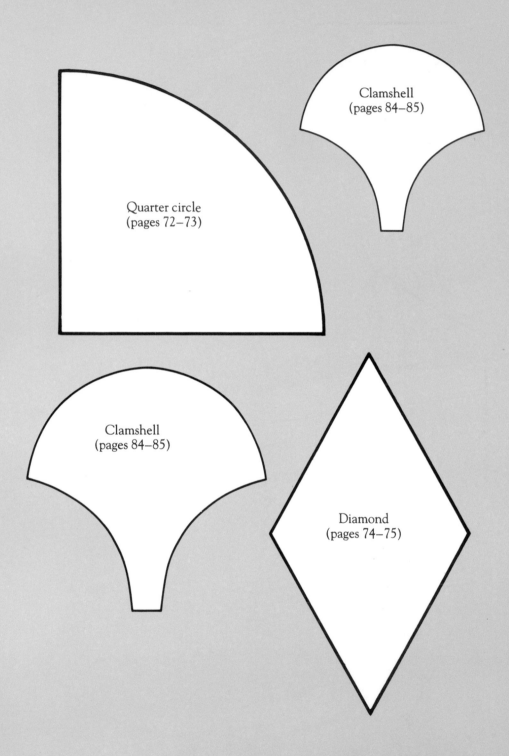

Quarter circle
(pages 72–73)

Clamshell
(pages 84–85)

Clamshell
(pages 84–85)

Diamond
(pages 74–75)

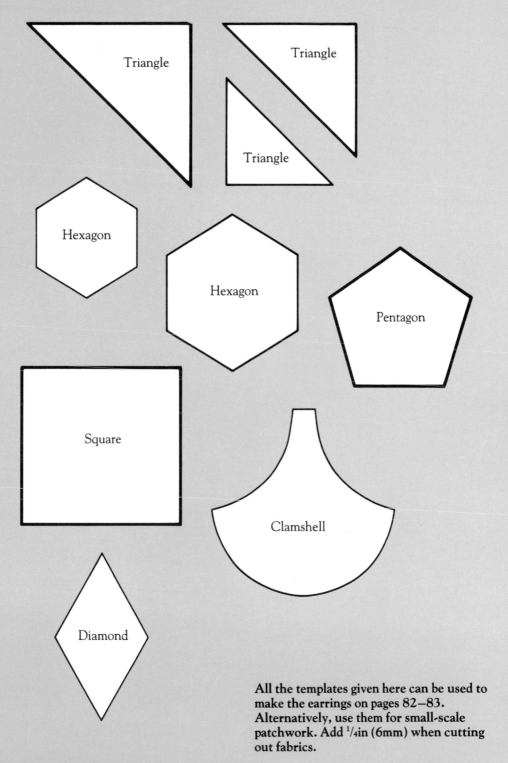

Triangle

Triangle

Triangle

Hexagon

Hexagon

Pentagon

Square

Clamshell

Diamond

All the templates given here can be used to make the earrings on pages 82–83. Alternatively, use them for small-scale patchwork. Add ¹⁄₄in (6mm) when cutting out fabrics.

1: HOUSE AND HOME

Puff of air

Suffolk puffs are traditionally used in quiltmaking because of the cosy pocket of trapped air inside each puff. Here they have been used to make a cushion cover trimmed with ribbon roses.

Materials

Cotton fabric, $2\frac{1}{2}$yd (228cm) × 36in (90cm) wide of dark yellow, $1\frac{1}{8}$yd (1m) × 36in (90cm) of light yellow
16 ribbon roses
Cushion pad, 16in (40cm) square

Preparation

1 Make a circular cardboard template, 3in (7.5cm) diameter.

2 Lay fabrics right side down on a flat surface and pencil round the template. Cut out 41 dark yellow circles and 40 light yellow circles.

3 Fold over the circle edges $\frac{1}{4}$in (6mm) and work running stitches all round.

4 Draw up gathering and secure with a back stitch. Flatten puffs in the fingers. Work all the puffs in the same way.

Making the cushion cover

5 Alternating the two yellows and working in rows of nine, catch puffs together on the wrong side with a few stitches.

6 When the patchwork is complete, cut two squares of dark yellow fabric to the same size as the patchwork plus $\frac{1}{2}$in (12mm) all round.

7 For the frill, cut and join pieces of the dark yellow fabric to make a strip 88 × 12in (224 × 30cm). Fold the strip in half lengthways and work two rows of gathering stitches along the raw edges.

8 Gather up the frill and pin evenly around one yellow square, right sides facing. Join ends of frill. Stitch frill in place.

9 Place two dark yellow squares with right sides together, sandwiching frill. Baste and stitch taking a $\frac{1}{2}$in (12mm) seam and leaving a gap for turning through. Turn cover, insert cushion pad and slipstitch gap.

10 Place patchwork to one side of cover. Pin in place, then catch puffs to cover around the edge. Sew on the ribbon roses.

> Suffolk puffs make ideal bedcovers. Cut 4in (10cm) circles from pre-shrunk cotton fabric, plain or patterned, or a mixture of both. Gather circles and sew together with the gathered sides uppermost.

Draw up the circle of fabric to form a puff

Sew the puffs together from the wrong side alternating dark and light yellows

Country garden

The hexagon is one of the most popular patchwork shapes. Simple to work and very pretty when finished, these placemats will grace your summer lunch tables.

Materials

Tracing paper
Cardboard for templates
Stiff notepaper for backing papers
Pieces of floral cotton fabric in three
    different designs (A, B, C) for each mat
Lining fabric, 12in (30cm) square for each
    mat

Preparation

1 Trace the large hexagon on page 8 and transfer the shape to cardboard. Use the template to cut 19 shapes from stiff notepaper. From the fabrics, cut 1 × A, 6 × B and 12 × C hexagons, adding ¼in (6mm) all round.

2 Pin a paper to the centre of each fabric hexagon. Turn over edges and baste, making clean, sharp corners.

Making the mats

3 Take one hexagon A as the centre and with right sides together, oversew a hexagon B to each of the six sides.

4 With right sides together, oversew the adjoining edges of the six hexagons. Work 12 C hexagons to the edges of mat.

Finishing

5 Press the patchwork and carefully snip the basting stitches holding the papers in place. Shake out the papers. Use the patchwork as a pattern for cutting the lining, adding an extra ¼in (6mm) for turnings.

6 Fold the edges under, cutting into the corners to ease folding. Oversew the lining to the patchwork.

Hexagon patchwork presents an uneven edge, which is attractive in itself but may not always be desired. To 'square off' hexagon patchwork, for mats or cloths, you need to cut half hexagons and triangles to fill the sides. Use the same template to cut 'filler' patches, remembering to add ¼in (6mm) seam allowance on the cut edge for neatening.

Fold fabric edges onto paper, folding sharp corners, baste

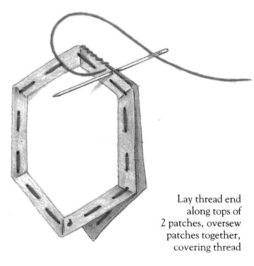

Lay thread end along tops of 2 patches, oversew patches together, covering thread

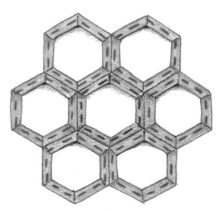

Oversew six patches round the central hexagon

17

Lunch for six

*This patchwork tablecloth is worked round a central hexagon rosette
then more hexagons are added to the corners to shape into a rectangle.*

Materials
For a cloth measuring 59 × 79in
(150 × 200cm)
Pieces of cotton fabric in eight different
designs (A–G)
Pink cotton tablecloth, 60 × 80in
(152 × 203cm)

Preparation
1 Trace and cut a template from the large
hexagon on page 8. Cut 229 paper
hexagons. Cut cotton fabric patches as
follows: 13 × A, 24 × B, 24 × C, 30 × D,
36 × E, 48 × F, 54 × G, adding ¼in (6mm)
all round each patch.

> **Grandmother's flower garden**
> Hexagons form one of the most popular
> quilt patterns. Traditionally, a yellow or
> orange hexagon is used for the central
> patch then surrounded with two or
> three rows of flower-patterned
> hexagons. Use plain green for the
> background.

Working the patchwork
2 To work the first round, begin with a
central hexagon A and oversew six B
hexagons to the sides.

3 Continue in rounds as follows: A, B, C, D
and E until the 6th round of 36 hexagons has
been completed.

4 Finish each corner with 12 F hexagons to
elongate the rosette into a rectangle.

5 Complete the patchwork with a border of
G hexagons around the edges. Remove the
backing paper.

Finishing the cloth
6 Place the patchwork in the centre of the
tablecloth and pin in place, making sure
that the edges are parallel.

7 Slipstitch the patchwork in place.

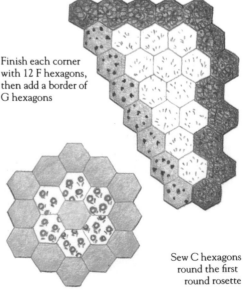

Finish each corner
with 12 F hexagons,
then add a border of
G hexagons

Sew C hexagons
round the first
round rosette

Somerset square

Somerset patchwork has a striking three-dimensional appearance. It is made by sewing folded rectangles on to a foundation fabric. Here it makes an elegant cushion cover.

Materials
Finished size 16in (40cm) square
Cotton fabrics, 36in (90cm) wide in the following amounts and colours:
1³/₄yd (170cm) plum
12in (30cm) each of pale pink and dusty pink
8¹/₂in (21cm) white print
5¹/₂in (14cm) each of plum print and cream print
Calico foundation fabric, 18in (45cm) square
Cushion pad, 16in (40cm) square

Preparation
1 From cotton fabric cut 2³/₄ × 4³/₄in (7 × 12cm) rectangles as follows: 24 plum, 20 pale pink, 16 dusty pink, 12 white print, 8 plum print, 4 cream print.

2 Fold a ¹/₄in (6mm) turning to the wrong side along one long edge of each rectangle.

3 Fold the top two corners to the middle of the lower edge and oversew through all layers to secure.

4 Mark the foundation square across the diagonals to find the centre.

Working the patchwork
5 Arrange the four cream print patches on the backing fabric with the points meeting at the centre, secure. Catch the points to the backing fabric.

6 Take the thread through the folds and secure the patches at the edges.

7 Arrange the next round of plum print patches overlapping the central four patches. Secure the patches to the backing.

Fold corners down to bottom edge of rectangle

Arrange four patches at the centre of the foundation square. Catch down points

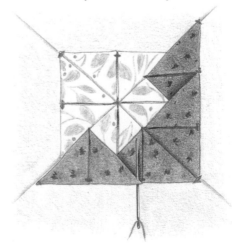

Arrange the next round of patches overlapping the first

8 Continue to add patches, working out from the centre point until the design is complete.

Making the cushion cover
9 Trim the foundation fabric to the size of the patchwork. Cut two plum fabric side border pieces 3 × 11in (8 × 28cm).

10 With right sides together, place side borders to patchwork edges and stitch, taking a ¹/₄in (6mm) seam, through all layers.

11 Cut two plum fabric borders 3in (8cm) wide to the width of the bordered patchwork and seam as for side borders.

12 From plum fabric cut a square to match the cushion front.

Finishing
13 Place the patchwork front to the back, right sides facing. Stitch on three sides. Turn right side out, insert cushion pad, close seam with slipstitches.

Somerset shimmer

This variation of Somerset patchwork makes each patch into a little sealed pocket. With a few sequins slipped into each one, this beautiful cushion cover takes on a shimmering quality with a delicate look.

Materials

Finished size 16in (40cm) square

Semi-sheer blue silk fabric, 24 × 36in (60 × 90cm)

Semi-sheer white polyester flock print, 18 × 36in (45 × 90cm)

Small packet of mixed colour sequins

White cotton backing fabric

Cushion pad

Preparation

1 From the blue silk, cut 20 pieces 5in (12.5cm) square. From white flock print, cut one 12in (30cm) square and fifteen 5in (12.5cm) squares.

2 Fold each square in half to form a rectangle. Fold the top corners to the centre and into each pocket drop three or four sequins. Seal the top of each patch by stitching across ¼in (6mm) from the open edges. Prepare all the patches in the same way.

Working the patchwork

3 Place the first row of blue patches from left to right on the flock square, ½in (12mm)

up from the lower edge (see illustration).

4 Sew the points in place, then run the thread through the folds and loosely catch the long edges to the flock fabric.

5 Work the second row of white flock fabric patches from right to left. Continue in this way until all rows are complete, working blue from left to right and white from right to left.

Make cushion cover

6 From blue silk, cut two 4in (10cm)-wide strips to the width of the patchwork. Fold the strips in half lengthways. Baste the folded edges to the sides of the patchwork and slipstitch together.

7 From blue silk, cut two 4in (10cm) wide strips to the depth of the bordered patchwork and slipstitch to each side.

8 Cut backing fabric to the size of the patchwork. Baste together right sides facing. Stitch on three sides, turn right side out. Insert cushion pad, close seam with slipstitches.

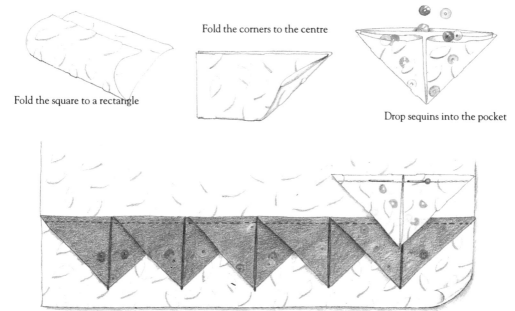

Fold the corners to the centre

Fold the square to a rectangle

Drop sequins into the pocket

Arrange five blue patches from left to right across bottom of foundation fabric, ½in (12mm) up from edge. Arrange second row of white patches from right to left

Time for tea

Take a break and prepare yourself for a tea-time treat with this extra-special tea cosy. The simple technique of using Somerset patches in-the-round forms an eye-catching central star motif.

Materials
Red cotton fabric, 40 × 60in (100 × 150cm)
Piece of red and white cotton print fabric
    18 × 36in (45 × 90cm)
Squared paper with 1in (2.5cm) squares
Piping cord, 30in (75cm) long
Heavyweight wadding, 20 × 60in
    (50 × 150cm)
Cotton lining, 20 × 60in (50 × 150cm)

Preparation
1 From red fabric cut 20 rectangles and from red and white fabric cut 24 rectangles
$1^3/_4$ × 3in (4.5 × 7.5cm).

2 Turn under the top edge of each rectangle by $^1/_4$in (6mm).

3 Fold the top corners to the middle to form a triangle, with raw edges level, and secure with small stitches at the lower edge.

4 Cut a 10in (25cm) foundation square from cotton lining. Mark the centre of the foundation square by creasing it diagonally.

5 Secure four red patches at the central point. Arrange the next eight patterned patches overlapping the first, but $^1/_2$in (12mm) from centre and spacing extra patches at the diagonals between the first round.

6 Continue to work in rounds, spacing the patches over the previous round and in-between until the design is complete.

Making the cosy
7 From the graph pattern on page 25, draw a pattern on squared paper. Use the pattern to cut out the tea cosy back and front from red fabric. Cut a circle from the cosy front to

Place first patch in position on foundation square

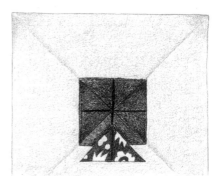

Position four patches, sew in place, then work
next round of patches $^1/_2$in (12mm) from middle

Fit patches in between to make the third round

24

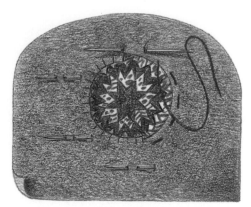

Place cut-out cosy front over patchwork

Place made up lining inside cosy

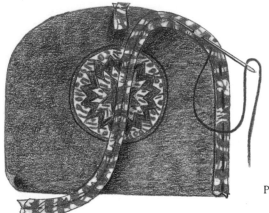

Baste piped cord round cosy front
Baste tab centre top.

frame the patchwork. Cut cosy back and front from lining and wadding.

8 Place the front over the star design and pin into place. Turn the edges of the circle under $^1/_4$in (6mm). Baste and then machine-stitch all round.

9 Cut a 30 × 1in (75 × 2.5cm) bias strip from the printed fabric. Fold strip in half with wrong sides together. Tuck piping cord inside and baste close to the cord to hold in place.

10 With raw edges level, arrange the piping cord around the right side of the cosy front.

11 Make a tab from $1^1/_2$ × 1in (4 × 2.5cm) bias strip. Fold with right sides together,

stitch a $^1/_4$in (6mm) seam and turn right side out. Baste the tab in place at centre front, facing downwards.

12 With right sides together stitch back and front cosy together round outer edge, taking a $^1/_4$in (6mm) seam. Clip curves and turn the cosy to the right side.

13 Stitch wadding pieces to lining pieces. Trim back wadding seam allowance. With right sides together, join back and front lining, but do not turn through. Place the lining bag inside the tea cosy.

14 Fold the edges of the lining to the inside. Fold the outer cosy edges $^1/_4$in (6mm) to the inside of the cosy and slipstitch over the lining.

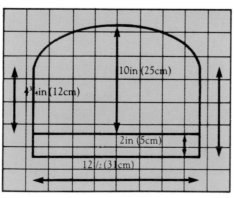

10in (25cm)

4³/₄in (12cm)

6³/₄in (17cm)

2in (5cm)

12¹/₂ (31cm)

Graph for teacosy
scale 1sq = 1in (2.5cm)

Window whispers

Inspired by traditional cathedral window patchwork, this curtain panel made of delicate muslin allows sunlight to shine through softly. The design is ideal for both full-length and café-style curtains.

Materials
For a 28¼ × 47¼in (72 × 120cm) panel
Cotton muslin, 4½yd (4m) × 40in (100cm)
Cotton lace, 1⅜yd (120cm) of ¾in
(2cm)-wide lace

Preparation
1 Fold muslin lengthways along the grain, matching selvedges. Draw a lengthways thread from the centre of the fabric to find the straight grain.

2 Cut fifteen 19½in (50cm) squares. Press ¼in (6mm) turnings on all four sides.

3 Fold each square across the diagonals and press lightly to form a crease marking the centre of the square.

4 Fold the corners of the square to the centre and secure with backstitches. Fold the new corners once again to the centre and secure with a backstitch. The square is now approximately half the original size.

Making up the panel
5 With right sides together, pin squares together in threes and oversew along the edges.

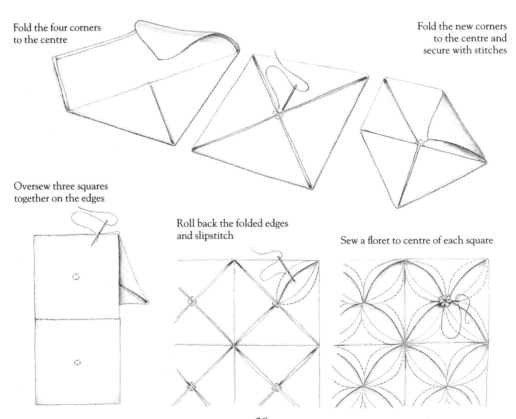

Fold the four corners to the centre

Fold the new corners to the centre and secure with stitches

Oversew three squares together on the edges

Roll back the folded edges and slipstitch

Sew a floret to centre of each square

28

6 Matching seams, join five strips together to make a block.

7 Roll back the folded edge of each square ¾in (18mm) at the widest point, tapering towards the corners. Press the edge, then slipstitch in place through all thicknesses.

8 Cut the lace into 15 pieces 3½in (8cm) long. Gather the lace along one edge and draw into a floret. Secure a floret to the centre of each square.

2: GIFT IDEAS

With love

Silky satin ribbons are perfect for delicate folded strip patchwork. There is no need to neaten the edges and they come in all the colours of the rainbow. These beautiful greetings cards make wonderful gifts and are an ideal way to display your patchwork.

Materials
Satin ribbon, 10in (24cm) of ³/₈in (1cm) wide in each of nine or ten colours
Pelmet-weight non-iron interfacing, 4in (10cm) square for each card
Thin card, glue

Preparation
1 Mark the centre of the interfacing square. Cut ribbons into pieces 2¹/₂in (6cm) long.

2 Fold the ribbon strips to make a point with the satin side uppermost. Press lightly with a cool iron to hold the point.

Working the patchwork
3 Beginning at the centre of the square, place four ribbons with points meeting. Catch the points down with a stitch.

4 Make three more stitches at the centre and ends of the ribbon as shown in the diagram.

5 Build up the next round of four patches, placing them ¹/₄in (6mm) below the first. Stitch in place. Continue to build up a star motif in rounds of four ribbons, alternating the colours for a pretty effect.

6 Cut one piece of card 6 × 8¹/₄in (15 × 21cm) and another piece 6 × 4¹/₈in (15 × 10.5cm). Fold the larger piece of card in half.

7 Use a pair of compasses to draw a circle on the front of the card to just under the patchwork diameter. Cut out the circle.

8 Place patchwork behind window and glue in place. Glue the smaller piece of card behind patchwork to neaten.

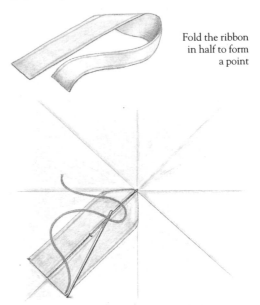

Fold the ribbon in half to form a point

Stitch the ribbon at the point, centre and ends

Build up the design in rounds of folded ribbon patches

32

Hostess with the mostest

Combine patchwork and frills to make this special occasion hostess apron. It will be a talking point the next time you entertain.

Materials
Brown cotton fabric, 2yd (1.8m) × 60in (150cm) wide

Floral cotton fabric in brown, green and blue, 10in × 45in (25 × 115cm) wide in each

Preparation
1 Trace the octagon on page 8 and transfer to card. Cut out for a template. Cut out 9 brown, 8 green and 7 blue patches adding $\frac{1}{4}$in (6mm) all round. Cut square, triangular and corner triangles templates in the same way. Cut out 13 brown squares, 18 brown edge triangles and 8 brown corner triangles again adding $\frac{1}{4}$in (6mm) all round.

2 Cut out the corresponding number of papers. Pin a paper to each piece of fabric and fold over the edges. Baste turnings.

Working the patchwork
3 Work rows of octagons with right sides facing, oversewing the edges.

4 When the rows of octagons are complete, join in the triangles along the lower edge, matching the points carefully.

5 Build up the blocks, working the larger patches first, then joining in the squares and triangles. Work the apron bib patchwork in the same way.

Making the apron
6 Cut two side apron borders $4\frac{1}{4}$in × 18in (11 × 46cm). Fold borders in half lengthways, press a $\frac{1}{4}$in (6mm) to wrong side on one long edge. With right sides together stitch borders to patchwork side taking a $\frac{1}{4}$in (6mm) seams (see illustration on page 36).

7 Cut a frill $5\frac{1}{2}$ × $38\frac{1}{2}$in (14 × 98cm) and

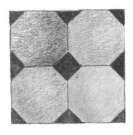

Colour and template plan for the bib and apron

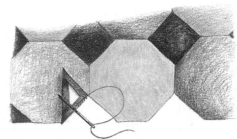

Join a triangle to an octagon with oversewing stitches

34

make a narrow hem on one long side. Work gathering stitches along the unhemmed edge of the frill and draw up to the width of the apron (including the side borders).

8 With right sides together, stitch the frill to the apron distributing the gathers evenly. Neaten the short edges of the frill.

9 Cut an apron lining $14^{1}/_{2} \times 18$in (37×46cm) and turn $^{1}/_{4}$in (6mm) under on the lower edge. With wrong sides together, slipstitch the lining to patchwork front using the hem stitching line as a guide.

10 Slipstitch the side borders in place over the apron lining.

11 Cut two waistband strips $2^{1}/_{2} \times 18^{1}/_{2}$in ($6 \times 47$cm). Mark the centre of the waistband, bib and apron front with a coloured thread. With right sides together, baste one waistband to the apron, matching the markers, and stitch a $^{1}/_{4}$in (6mm) seam.

12 Cut a bib border $4^{1}/_{4} \times 7^{1}/_{2}$in ($11 \times 19$cm) and fold in half lengthways. With right sides together, stitch border to bib taking a $^{1}/_{4}$in (6mm) seam.

13 Cut the bib lining $7^{1}/_{2}$in (19cm) square. Turn under top edge by $^{1}/_{4}$ (6mm) and slipstitch in place to top bib seam.

14 Cut two side bib borders $4^{1}/_{4} \times 7^{1}/_{2}$in ($11 \times 19$cm). Cut two straps $4^{1}/_{4} \times 12^{1}/_{4}$in ($11 \times 31$cm). Join side bib borders together with the straps to form one piece.

15 Press open the seams. With right sides together, place the borders each side of the bib and stitch in place along one edge of each border. Turn under opposite edge of border by $^{1}/_{4}$in (6mm) and slipstitch to lining through all the layers.

16 With right sides together, and matching markers, stitch the bib to the front waistband.

17 Turn under the second waistband piece by $^{1}/_{4}$in (6mm) and slipstitch to bodice and apron seams.

18 Fold the strap and bib borders to match turnings and oversew along the edges.

19 Join the top edges of the waistbands together either side of the bib.

20 Cut two ties $3 \times 26^{1}/_{2}$in (8×67cm) and turn a $^{1}/_{4}$in (6mm) hem along the two long and one short edge of each tie. Stitch. Pleat the other end of each tie and insert into open end of waistband. Slipstitch in place.

Stitch the border strip to the apron, right sides together and taking a $^{1}/_{4}$in (6mm) seam

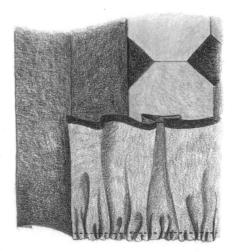

Join the frill to the lower edge of the apron with machine-stitching. Then neaten the short ends.

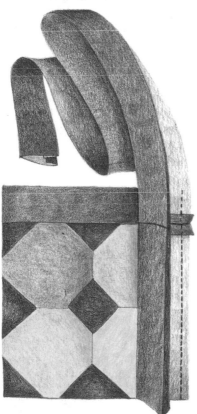

Join one edge of the border to the bib

Pleat the end of tie and insert into the waistband

Clam bake

Heavy quality upholstery fabrics can also be used for creating patchwork. Here they have been combined in overlapping clamshells to make an attractive oven mitt that would make a useful gift.

Materials
Heavyweight cotton furnishing fabric
Medium-weight non-iron interfacing
Graph paper with 1in (2.5cm) squares
Cotton backing fabric, 12in (30cm) square
Medium-weight polyester wadding
Cotton lining fabric, 12 × 18in (30 × 45cm)
Calico, 12in (30cm) square
Matching bias binding

Preparation
1 Trace the large clamshell on page 9 to make a card template and cut out 16 patterns in interfacing.

2 Using the same template, cut 16 clamshells in upholstery fabric adding ¼in (6mm) all round.

3 Baste the fabric and interfacing clamshells together, turning the curved edge turning to the wrong side. Gather the fabric so that the curved, top edge is smooth (see illustration on opposite page).

Working the patchwork
4 Draw a mitt pattern from the graph and trace the shape on to the backing fabric. Place the first three clamshells at the top of the mitt and work hemming or slipstitches along the curved edges, through to the backing (see illustration). Place clamshell 4 in position under clamshell 1 and overlapping 2 and 3. Hem or slipstitch in place.

5 Continue to build up rows of clamshells in the same way, making sure that the tops of the curved edges are aligned.

To make the mitt
6 Cut out the mitt pattern and cut two in cotton lining, one each in wadding and calico. Cut out the patchwork.

7 Baste wadding to the wrong side of patchwork. Baste calico to wadding, stitch all round. Trim seam allowance bind all round. Make up lining, slip into mitt, turn wrist edges and catch to inside.

Graph pattern for the oven mitt. Scale 1sq = 1in (2.5cm)

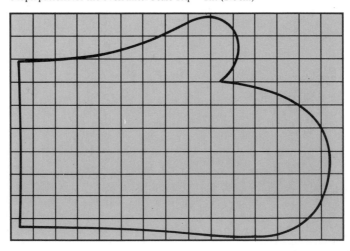

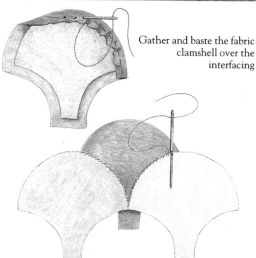

Gather and baste the fabric
clamshell over the
interfacing

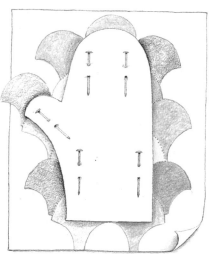

Sew clamshells together on the curved edges
using small stitches

Use the paper pattern to cut out the patchwork

It's a gem

Even the smallest scraps of beautiful fabrics can be saved to create patchwork designs. This jewellery roll uses tiny pieces of Liberty lawn to bring alive a cotton mini-print.

Materials
One piece each of plain and patterned
   cotton fabric
Blue cotton fabric for lining
Patterned cotton fabric for inside of roll
Two zips, 5in (13cm) long
Black velvet cord, 50in (125cm) long
One button

Preparation
1 Trace the triangle on page 9 and transfer on to cardboard. Cut out for a template. Use the template to cut 24 paper triangles. Cut 12 fabric triangles in each of the two designs, adding ¼in (6mm) all round.

2 Pin papers to the wrong side of fabric triangles. Fold over the edges and baste. To make the corners neat, fold them twice and secure with a stitch.

Making the roll
3 Pair up and oversew the plain and patterned triangles together to make 12 squares, sewing along the diagonal edges (see picture on opposite page).

4 Sew the squares into a block of 4 × 3 squares. Press, remove basting and shake out papers.

5 Cut one piece of blue fabric 6½ × 9in (16.5 × 23cm). Cut two pieces in blue and two in patterned fabric, 6½ × 4½in (16.5 × 11.5cm). Turn under ½in (12mm) along one long edge of each of the four smaller pieces.

6 To assemble the jewellery roll, place the larger piece of blue fabric right side up. Place two patterned pieces of fabric right side down at each end, then two blue pieces of fabric on top right sides up, matching raw edges. Baste and stitch around edge through all layers taking a ¼in (6mm) seam. Turn roll to right side.

Hand-sew the doubled
zip to the centre
of the roll

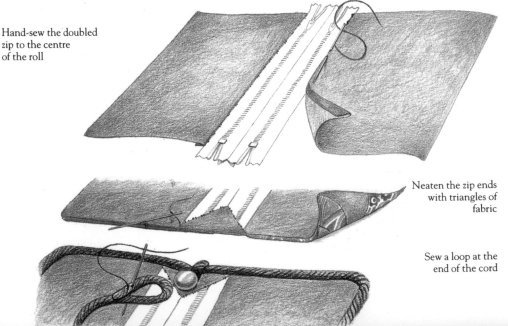

Neaten the zip ends
with triangles of
fabric

Sew a loop at the
end of the cord

7 Turn under edges of patchwork and pin to one end of roll. Slipstitch in place along the edges.

8 Join the zips together along the edges to form a double zip. Pin zip tapes in place under neatened edges of patterned fabric. Hand-sew in place and catch the centre of the double zip to the centre of roll. Neaten the zip ends with a triangle of fabric (see illustration on opposite page).

Finishing
9 Edge the jewellery roll with black velvet cord, oversewing it in place. Ease the cord around the corners. Sew cord along the spine.

10 For the centre spine, cut a piece of cord the length of the jewellery roll and make a small loop at one end. Sew the cord to one end of the centre spine and sew a button at the other end for the loop.

Pins and needles

Log cabin is one of the most popular American patchwork techniques. The design represents the structure of a log cabin built around a central chimney block with light and dark fabrics, depicting firelight and shadow on the cabin walls. Here, Log cabin makes a pretty pincushion.

Materials
Pieces of light and dark patterned cotton fabric
Foundation fabric, 5in (13cm) square
Backing fabric, 5in (13cm) square
Polyester washable toy filling

Preparation
1 Crease the foundation fabric diagonally to find the centre point. Cut the patterned cotton fabric into $1\frac{1}{4}$in (3cm)-wide strips.

2 Cut a $1\frac{1}{4}$in (3cm) 'chimney' square and set in the centre of the foundation square, matching the corners with the diagonal lines. Baste all round through both layers.

3 With right sides together, baste a light patterned strip to the top edge of the central piece. Sew in place by hand or machine, taking a $\frac{1}{4}$in (6mm) seam. Turn back the strip to the right side and lightly press.

4 With right sides together, baste a light patterned strip down the right-hand side of the first strip and central square. Sew into place taking a $\frac{1}{4}$in (6mm) seam then turn the strip to the right side and press.

5 Continue in this way along the remaining two edges of the square using dark patterned strips. Work three rounds of light and dark patterned strips to complete the block.

Finishing
6 With right sides together, sew the patchwork to the backing fabric, leaving a small gap for turning through.

7 Turn the cushion right side out, pad with toy filling and slipstitch the gap closed.

8 A larger pincushion can be made by using a bigger piece of foundation fabric and adding more strips all round.

Sew the first light strip on the top edge

Sew the second light strip down the right-hand side

Add the first dark strip along the bottom edge

The fourth strip on the left-hand edge completes first round

Sweet and simple

Filled with aromatic dried flowers and sweet-smelling herbs these attractive little sachets are ideal for slipping into a linen drawer or looping around a coathanger to hang in the wardrobe. Filled with wadding they could also make lovely pincushions.

POINTED STAR

Materials
Pieces of patterned and plain cotton fabric
Heavyweight interfacing
Ribbon or bead string
Buttons or beads
Dried flowers or herbs
Matching sewing thread

Preparation
1 Trace the diamond shape from page 9 and
cut 12 'papers' from interfacing. Cut 12
diamonds from fabric, adding ¼in (6mm) all
round.

2 Pin fabric shapes to interfacing. Fold
fabric edges on to interfacing, folding sharp
corners as shown in the illustrations. Baste
to secure.

To make the sachet
3 With right sides facing, sew six diamonds
together to form a star. Make a second star.

4 Sew a button or bead to the front of the
star. If the button has a shank, sink it into
the centre of the star and anchor it at the
back with a short piece of matchstick so that
it sits well down. Alternatively, pull the
bead well down on the thread, and secure on
the wrong side.

5 With right sides facing, sew back and
front together leaving ¼in (6mm) at the top
of each point to work after turning star
through. Leave a gap of two points for
turning. Turn to right side.

6 Fill with herbs or dried flowers. Slipstitch
to close the gap in the seam and enclose a
loop of beads or ribbon for hanging.
Decorate with beads.

> By using the larger hexagon on page 8 or
> the diamond on page 10, cushions can be
> made. The Starboard pattern (see page
> 47) makes a hexagon when the diamonds
> are sewn together. Several of these
> hexagons could be joined to make a
> complete quilt of diamonds.

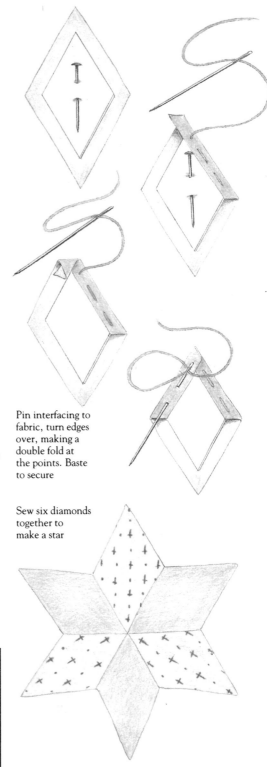

Pin interfacing to
fabric, turn edges
over, making a
double fold at
the points. Baste
to secure

Sew six diamonds
together to
make a star

45

HEXAGON SACHET

Materials
Pieces of plain and patterned cotton fabric
Pieces of interfacing
Ribbon or beading
Beads or seed pearls
Dried flowers or herbs
Matching sewing thread

Preparation
1 Trace the small hexagon on page 9 to make a cardboard template and cut out 14 interfacing patches.

2 Use the template to cut 14 fabric patches, adding ¼in (6mm) all round.

3 Fold and baste the fabric edges on to the interfacing (refer to page 17).

To make the sachet
4 With right sides together, oversew six patches around a central hexagon using tiny oversewing stitches.

5 With right sides facing, stitch the back and front together leaving a small gap for turning.

Finishing
6 Turn the sachet to the right side and stuff with herbs or dried flowers. Slipstitch to close the gap, tucking in a ribbon or beading loop for hanging.

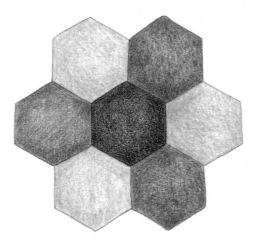

Sew six hexagons
round the central hexagon

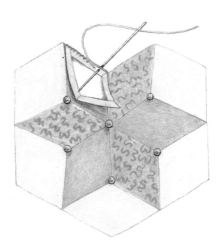

Sew diamond shapes into the
angles between the six diamonds

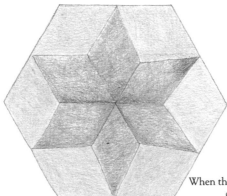

When the patchwork is complete, twelve
diamonds make a hexagon shape

STARBOARD

Materials
As for the Pointed star on page 45.

Preparation
Follow steps 1–3 as for the Pointed star.

4 Cut twelve more diamonds from interfacing. Cut twelve fabric diamonds adding ¹/₄in (6mm) seam allowance.

5 Mount the fabric diamonds on the interfacing. With right sides together, sew six diamonds round the edges of each pointed star (see illustration on opposite page).

6 Sew back and front together, leaving a gap for turning. Turn through to right side and fill with herbs or dried flowers.

7 Slipstitch the gap, enclosing a loop of beads or a ribbon for hanging.

Weekend break

Even an overnight stay calls for a roomy purse to hold lotions and potions. This attractive make-up bag is worked in cathedral patchwork which is self-lined, making it a hardwearing fabric.

Materials
Pieces of lavender cotton fabric
Pieces of lavender print cotton fabric
Pieces of rust cotton fabric
White zip fastener, 12in (30cm) long

Preparation
1 From lavender fabric cut out 18 patches 5¹/₂in (14cm) square and 13 window patches 1¹/₂in (4cm) square.

2 From lavender print cut 12 patches 5¹/₂in (14cm) square and 20 window patches 1¹/₂in (4cm) square.

3 From rust fabric cut 16 window patches 1¹/₂in (4cm) square.

4 Turn under ¹/₄in (6mm) along the edges of the large squares. Fold the corners to meet at the centre and secure with backstitches through all layers (see page 28).

5 Fold the new corners to the centre and secure again with stitches at the centre, through all layers. (The square should measure approximately half the original size.) Refer to page 28.

Making the bag
6 Join five squares together right sides facing (see page 28). Join the six strips of five squares together to complete the block (see illustration below).

7 Pin the patterned window squares in place (see illustration below, right). (There is no need to neaten the edges of the window squares as they will be covered by the edges of the foundation squares.)

8 Secure the window patches by folding back the foundation square over the window to ¹/₄in (6mm) at the widest point and tapering to the corners.

9 Stitch the folded edge into place, through all layers of fabric.

Finishing
10 Fold the patchwork in half, wrong sides together and slipstitch the side seams.

11 From the right side, pin the zip fastener into place just within the top edges so as not to show and slipstitch through all layers to secure.

Fold back the foundation square on to the window patch and sew in place through all layers

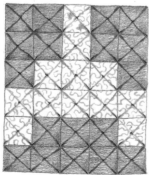

Join five squares in a strip, then six strips together

The patterned window patches are set between the squares

49

Heaven scent

Filled with lavender or pot-pourri, these pretty pomanders make attractive gifts to hang in the wardrobe or slip between clothes in a drawer. The pomanders are made from pentagon-shaped patches, all cut from the same fabric.

Materials
Pieces of pretty cotton fabrics
Ribbon
Pot-pourri or lavender

Preparation
1 Trace the pentagon on page 9 and transfer to cardboard. Use the template to cut 12 paper pentagons. Cut the same number of fabric pentagons, adding ¼in (6mm) all round.

2 Pin a paper centrally on each fabric pentagon, fold over the fabric edges and baste to secure.

Making a pomander
3 Take one pentagon as the base and oversew a pentagon to each side of the five sides (see illustration) Press the patchwork.

4 Oversew all the adjacent sides together. Work the other half of the pomander in the same way. Snip the basting threads and shake out the papers.

5 With right sides facing, sew the two halves together, leaving a gap for filling.

Finishing
6 Turn through and fill the pomander with pot-pourri or lavender. Insert a ribbon loop and slipstitch to close the gap.

More ideas for pentagon balls
To make Christmas tree baubles, use card instead of paper and leave the card in place after sewing up is completed. The last seam will have to be done from the right side. Use shiny and glittering fabrics, sew on gold or silver braids along the seams. Trim the balls with beads and sequins.

Soft baby balls
Draw round the pentagon template to enlarge the size. Cut shapes from soft, washable fabrics and sew together to make stuffed toy balls for babies.
  A bell can be pushed into the ball while stuffing. Make sure all seams are securely finished off to prevent them from opening and stuffing seeping out.

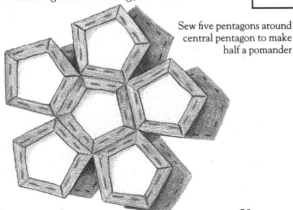

Sew five pentagons around central pentagon to make half a pomander

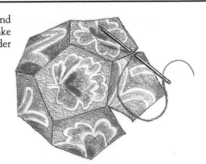

Sew two half pomanders together, leaving 2 sides open for filling.

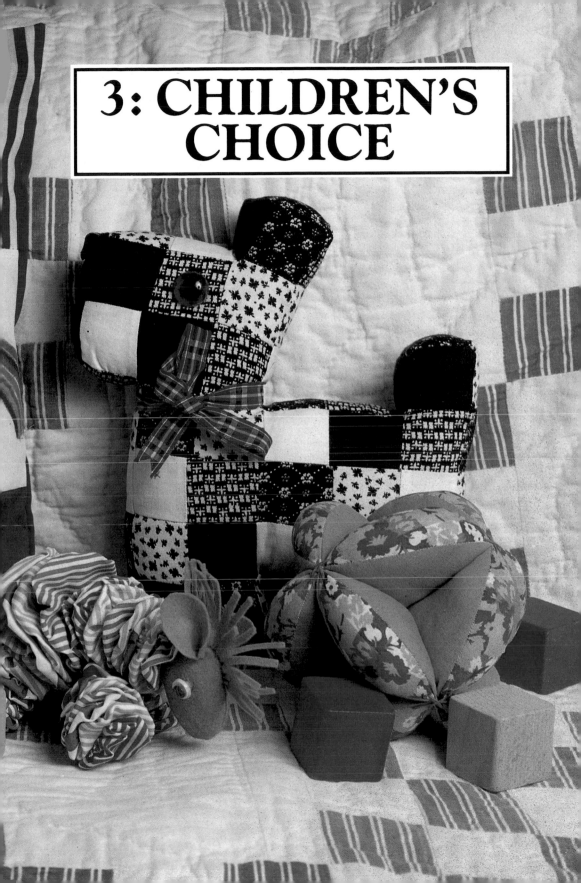

3: CHILDREN'S CHOICE

Work of art

Your children can help design their own quilt by drawing pictures on the plain white squares. Add colourful patches of plain and checked fabrics to complete a bedcover that they will treasure for years.

Materials

For a single bed quilt $51^1/_2 \times 90$in
  (131×228cm)
Cotton fabric, 36in (90cm) wide in the
  following lengths:
  30in (75cm) each of green and blue
  gingham
  10in (25cm) each of pink, green and blue
  50in (125cm) white
Blue cotton/polyester sheeting, $57 \times 95^1/_2$in
  (145×242cm)
Medium-weight wadding, $51^1/_2 \times 90$in
  (131×228cm)
Fabric crayons
Matching sewing thread

Preparation

1 From cotton fabrics cut 10in (25cm)
squares as follows: 7 pink gingham, 8 green
gingham, 7 blue gingham, 3 pink, 3 blue, 2
green and 15 white.

2 Practise the designs for the picture squares
on paper before working on the fabric.
When you are happy with the design, draw
pictures on each of the 15 white squares
using fabric crayons. Fix the colours with an
iron following the manufacturer's
instructions.

Working the patchwork

3 Following the layout for the quilt in the
picture, make up the squares in nine strips of
five patches, taking a $^1/_2$in (12mm) seam.
Join the nine strips together.

4 Turn under $^1/_2$in (12mm) on all edges of
the blue sheeting. Pin the patchwork
centrally to the piece of wadding, then place
in the centre of the blue sheeting.

5 Fold over the two side edges of the blue
sheeting to cover the sides of the patchwork.
Pin, baste and stitch through all layers. Fold
over the two ends in the same way and stitch
in place.

6 Following the seam lines of the patchwork
squares, work running stitches through all
layers.

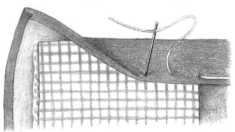

Fold over side edges,
baste through all layers

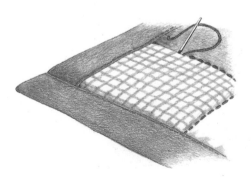

Work running stitches
along seam lines

Edward bear

Our traditional jointed teddy bear is made from antique patchwork, but a modern equivalent would look just as good. Make your own patchwork from madras cotton or other patterned fabrics.

Materials
Squared graph paper
Approx 39in (1m) square of patchwork
4 white buttons, ¹/₂in (12mm) diameter
Safety toy eyes, ³/₈in (9mm) diameter
Washable polyester toy filling
Ribbon, 39in (1m) long
Long, double-ended upholstery needle

Preparation
1 Prepare the patchwork, press and remove the papers.

2 From the trace-off patterns on pages 58–62, draw and cut out the pattern pieces, making sure that the pieces are reversed where necessary for matching opposite sides.

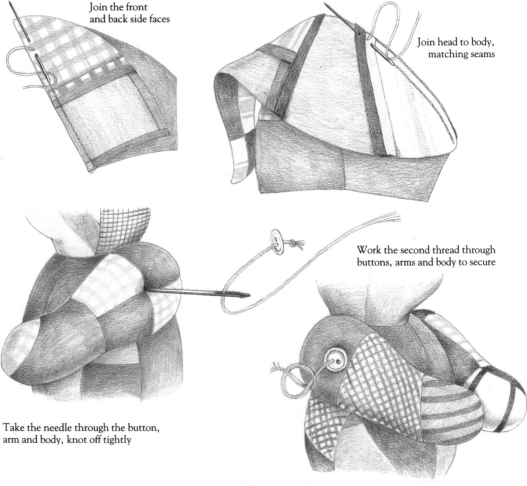

Join the front and back side faces

Join head to body, matching seams

Work the second thread through buttons, arms and body to secure

Take the needle through the button, arm and body, knot off tightly

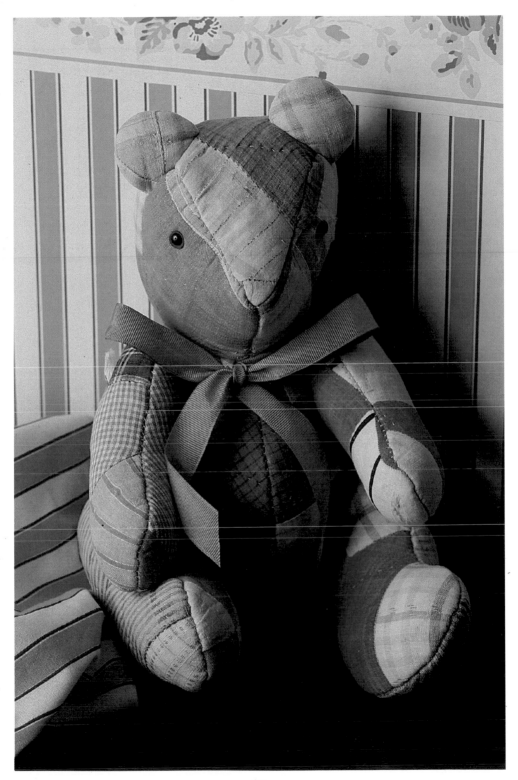

Edward bear

Trace the shapes on these pages and pages 60–62. Cut from the fabric as instructed. A seam allowance of ¼in (6mm) has been included.

Use the patterns to cut pieces from patchwork fabric.

Making the bear

3 Beginning with the head and with right sides together, join the front and back side faces from nose to neck.

4 With right sides together and starting at the nose, join head piece to the side faces.

5 Join the centre back and centre front body seams. With right sides together, join the back to the front at side seams, leaving a gap in one seam for turning through.

6 With right sides together, join the head to the body, matching the front and side seams. Secure the safety eyes in place.

7 Turn the teddy right side out and stuff firmly with the wadding, moulding the bear into shape. Slipstitch the opening in seam.

8 With right sides facing, sew the ears

together in pairs around curved edge. Turn out and gently pad. Slipstitch straight edge. Sew ears into place on top of head.

9 With right sides together sew the arms in pairs leaving a gap for turning through. Pad the arms and slipstitch opening. Make legs in the same way.

10 Thread the upholstery needle with several strands of cotton and make a firm knot at one end.

11 Thread the needle through the button and then through the arm and body. Pull tightly and thread the needle through the other arm and button. Pull the threads tightly and secure with a firm knot. Trim ends of threads. Thread a second group of threads through the second hole in each button.

12 Secure the legs in the same way. Tie a ribbon bow around the neck. If the toy is for a child, sew the ribbon on securely.

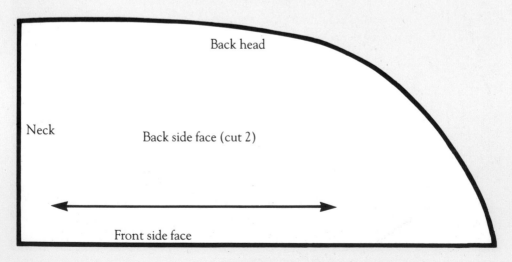

Back head

Neck

Back side face (cut 2)

Front side face

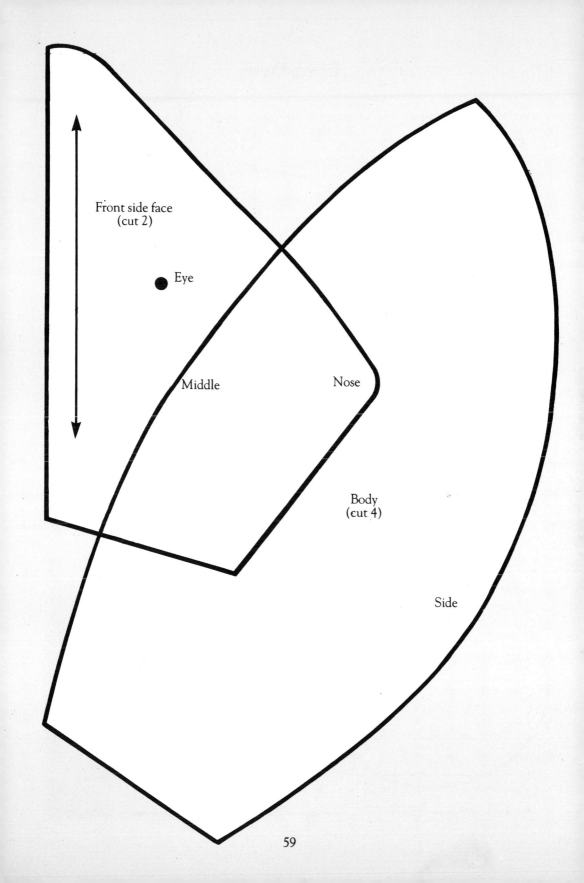

Front side face
(cut 2)

● Eye

Middle

Nose

Body
(cut 4)

Side

59

Edward bear

Trace-off shapes for the arm, ear and head.

Join to body

Arm (cut 4)

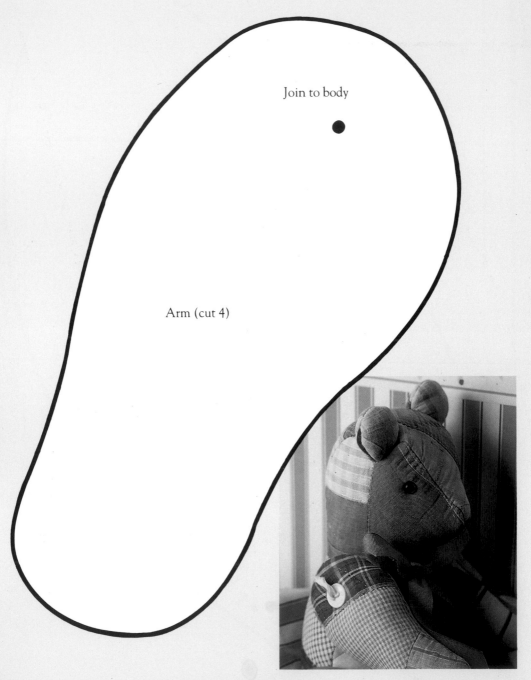

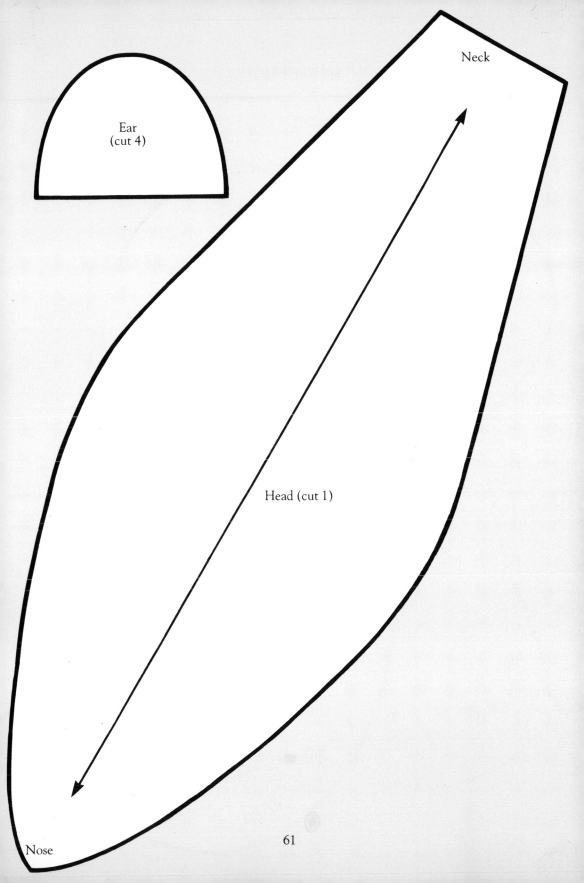

Ear
(cut 4)

Neck

Head (cut 1)

Nose

Edward bear

Trace-off shape for the bear's leg.

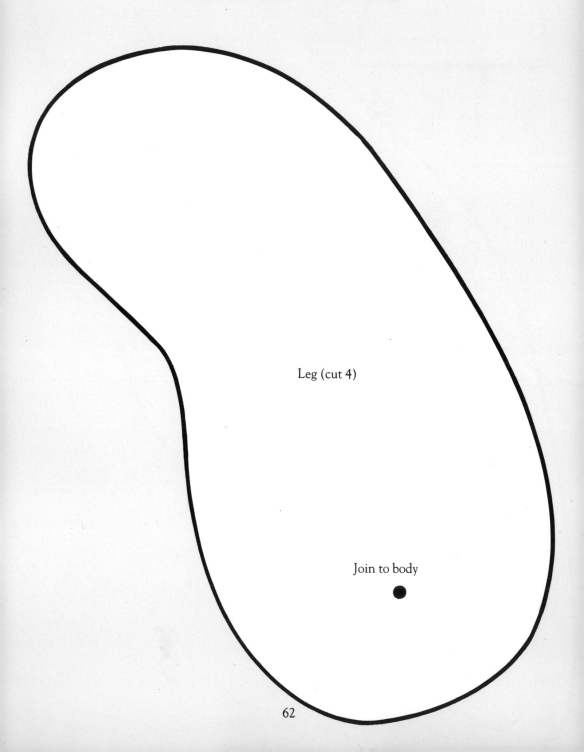

Leg (cut 4)

Join to body

Puffin pet

Suffolk puffs are traditionally sewn on to a backing fabric to make cushions and quilts but these simple shapes can also be threaded on to elastic to make simple soft toys, like this little horse.

Other toys, such as clown dolls, can be made with puffs

Materials
Pieces of red, yellow, pink, blue and green striped fabric
Cord elastic, 1yd (90cm) long
Turquoise felt square
Safety toy eyes, $\frac{1}{2}$in (12mm) diameter
Washable polyester toy filling

Preparation
1 Use a pair of compasses to make two circular templates, 6in (15cm) and 4in (10cm) diameter.

2 From striped fabric, cut out eight large circles and 41 small circles. turn under $\frac{1}{4}$in (6mm) to wrong side around edge of each circle.

3 Using double stranded thread, work running stitches around edge of each circle. Pull the threads to gather up each puff and tie the ends to secure.

Making the toy
4 Tie a knot in the end of the elastic and thread on eight large puffs. Tie a second knot to secure, allowing space for the puffs to expand.

5 Make four legs in the same way, using eight small circles for each leg. Make the neck using nine small circles. Tie the front legs and the neck to the body elastic, one puff in from the end. Tie the other pair of legs to the opposite end of the body, one puff in from the end.

Finishing
6 Trace the head, ears and mane from the pattern. From felt, cut out two ears, two heads and one mane. Cut a 5 × 2in (10 × 4cm) strip for the tail. Place head pieces together and stitch a $\frac{1}{4}$in (6mm) seam, leaving a small gap for turning. Turn right side out. Secure the eyes. Stuff lightly with filling and slipstitch gap.

7 Fringe the edge of the mane. Sew lower edge of mane to head, as shown in the picture on page 63, gathering slightly to fit.

8 Fold base of each ear in half and sew to either side of head. Sew head to neck at end puff.

9 Cut fringe in tail. Roll straight end of tail into a tube and slipstitch edge to hold. Stitch tail to large puff at end of body.

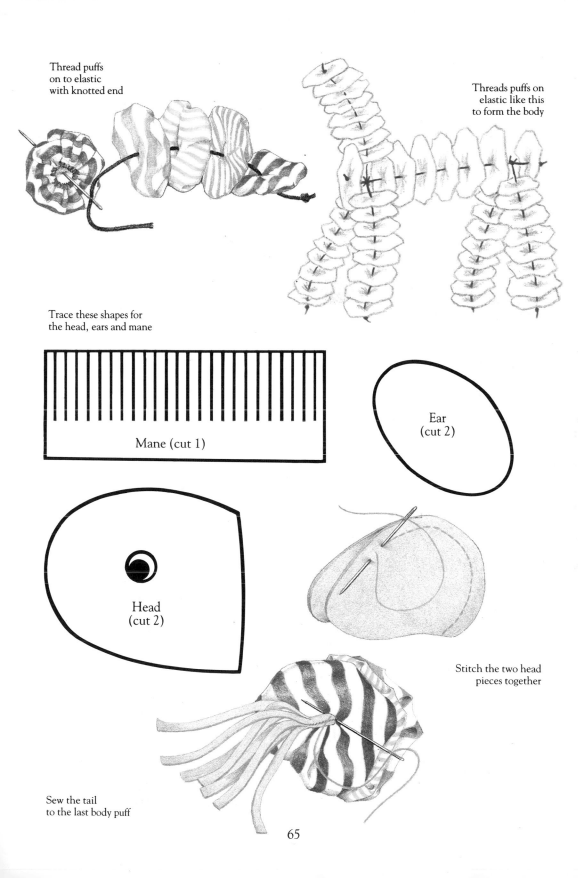

Thread puffs
on to elastic
with knotted end

Threads puffs on
elastic like this
to form the body

Trace these shapes for
the head, ears and mane

Mane (cut 1)

Ear
(cut 2)

Head
(cut 2)

Stitch the two head
pieces together

Sew the tail
to the last body puff

All-square

This smart, cot-sized duvet cover is made using one of the simplest patchwork techniques. The choice of plain and patterned fabrics in a limited range of colours makes for a smart effect.

Materials

For a 47¼ × 35¼in (120 × 90cm) cot cover
Navy dot cotton fabric, 18 × 48in
  (45 × 122cm)
Cotton fabric in burgundy stripe, trellis
  pattern and beige stripe, 12 × 48in
  (30 × 122cm) of each
Navy cotton fabric, 12 × 60in (30 × 150cm)
Cotton sateen lining, 1⅛yd (1m) × 60in
  (150cm)
5 large press fasteners
Matching sewing thread

Preparation

1 Make a cardboard template 4½in (11cm)
square. Cut out 88 squares of patterned
cotton fabric as follows: 25 navy dot, 22
burgundy stripe, 21 trellis pattern and 20
beige stripe.

2 Draw and cut a cardboard template 4in
(10cm) square and use it to cut out 88 paper
templates. Pin a paper centrally to the
wrong side of each fabric square.

3 Fold over opposite edges of each square
then fold down top edge and secure with a
small stitch in the corners and in the middle
of each folded side. Turn up the bottom edge
and secure in the same way.

4 From navy cotton, cut out two pieces A
and C 2¼ × 36in (6 × 91cm), and two
pieces B and D 2¼ × 44in (6 × 112cm).

Working the patchwork

5 Following the plan, arrange patches in
rows on the work surface. Turn them over
one by one, and number them on the paper
backing.

6 With right sides together, oversew squares
together in widthways strips of eight
patches, making sure the corner folds do not
catch in the stitches.

7 Matching seams, join the 11 strips together along the long edges. Snip the basting
stitches and shake to remove the papers.

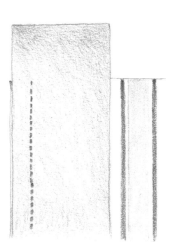

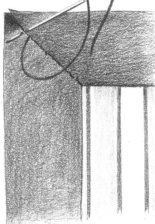

Join the side strips, right sides facing   Fold and mitre corners, sew by hand using neat stitches

Assembling the cover

8 With right sides together, pin and baste strip B to the left hand edge of the patchwork, taking ¼in (6mm) seam. Press to the right side. Join strip D to opposite edge in the same way.

9 Join strips A and C to the top and bottom edges. Fold and mitre the corners and sew by hand.

10 Cut the lining fabric into two pieces, one for the flap 36 × 11½in (91 × 29cm) and one for the main piece 36 × 38in (91 × 96.5cm).

11 Stitch a ⅜in (9mm) hem on the opening edges.

12 Press out the side strips of the patchwork front. With right sides together, pin and baste main lining piece to patchwork front. Pin and baste lining flap in place, overlapping main piece. Stitch, taking a ¼in (6mm) seam.

13 Turn the cover to the right side and mark positions for five press fasteners along the opening. Attach the press studs.

Baby-sized duvet cover
Use a large, frilled pillow case as a basis for an appliquéd duvet cover. Cut patchwork shapes from fabric, mount them on Vilene and attach to the cover.

Crayon cushion

Capture your children's earliest drawings in this sunny cushion cover or use fabric crayons to create your own designs and combine them with primary coloured patches for this colourful cushion.

Materials

Five coloured and four white fabric patches, 6¼in (16cm) square
Fabric crayons
Plain cotton fabric, ⅝yd (50cm) square
Cushion pad, 16in (40cm) square

Preparation

1 Practise your drawings on paper before working directly on to the fabric. Keep the designs simple and bold. When you are pleased with the picture draw the designs on to the white fabric squares using fabric crayons.

2 To 'fix' the colours, set the iron temperature according to the instructions for the crayons. Place a piece of paper over the design and iron for approximately 30 seconds.

Working the patchwork

3 Arrange the picture squares with the coloured fabric squares and pin together in strips of three. With right sides together, baste and stitch the patches together taking ¼in (6mm) seams.

4 Press seams open and pin the three strips together, matching seams. Baste and stitch.

5 Cut a cushion back to the same size as front. With right sides together machine-stitch all round three sides, leaving one side open to insert the cushion pad.

6 Trim the corners of the seams diagonally and turn the cover to the right side. Insert the cushion pad and slipstitch to close the opening.

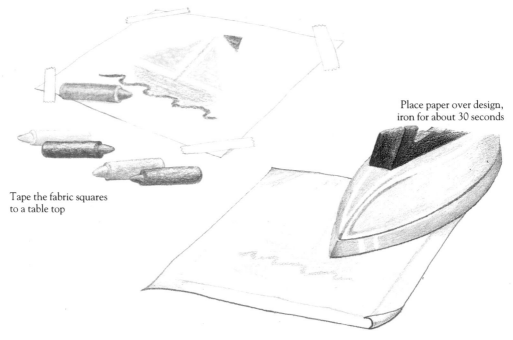

Place paper over design, iron for about 30 seconds

Tape the fabric squares to a table top

Scottie dog

Black and white patchwork looks wonderfully dramatic. From just a few remnants of fabric you can create this soft Scottie dog complete with a traditional tartan ribbon collar.

Materials
Pieces of plain white and black cotton fabric, plus three contrasting patterned fabrics
Safety toy eyes, $^3/_4$in (18mm) diameter
Safety dog nose
Polyester toy filling
Tartan ribbon, $^5/_8$in (15mm) wide × 24in (60cm)
Matching sewing thread

Preparation
1 Cut out 2in (5cm) squares of cotton fabric as follows: 20 black squares, and 16 squares each of white, leaf print, check and trellis print.

Making the dog
2 Following the layout plan, make up the front of the dog in strips of patchwork squares sewing $^1/_4$in (6mm) seams.

3 Sew the strips together to form one piece, matching the seams. Assemble the back piece in the same way.

4 Join a strip of 30 squares, to form the gusset which goes right round the dog.

5 Matching seams, pin and baste the gusset to the front piece of the dog, right sides facing. Stitch a $^1/_4$in (6mm) seam. Sew the back piece to the gusset in the same way, right sides facing, leaving part of the seam open for stuffing.

6 Attach the safety eyes and nose to the head. Turn the dog right side out and stuff firmly with filling. Close the opening in the seam with slipstitches.

Finishing
7 Tie a ribbon bow around the dog's neck.

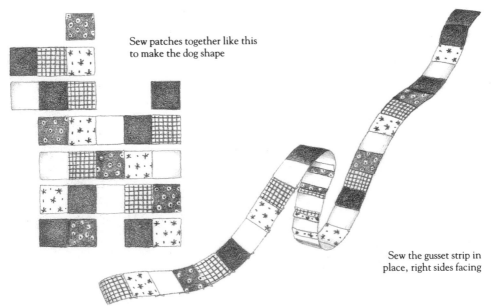

Sew patches together like this to make the dog shape

Sew the gusset strip in place, right sides facing

Bouncing ball

This colourful ball is one of the simplest and safest toys for a baby. Cleverly constructed from quarter circles and segments, the ball is perfect for tiny hands to grip.

Materials
Pieces of plain and printed cotton fabric
Washable polyester toy filling

Preparation
1 Trace the shapes on pages 9 and 10 and transfer to card. Cut out for templates. Cut 12 patterned cotton ellipses and 24 plain cotton quarter circles adding $1/4$in (6mm) seam allowance all round.

2 Use the templates to cut out the same number of paper shapes.

3 Pin a paper centrally to the wrong side of each fabric patch. Fold fabric edges over the papers and baste.

Making the ball
4 With right sides together, oversew a quarter circle to each side of an ellipse.

5 Oversew the straight sides leaving an opening in one side for turning through.

6 Remove the papers, and turn segments through to the right side. Pad with toy filling and slipstitch the gap closed.

7 Place four segments at right angles and stitch together at the top and bottom. Join four more segments together in the same way.

8 Join the four centre segments together at the centre and outer points.

9 Sandwich the centre layer between the top and lower sections and stitch at the points where they meet.

10 Work two buttonhole loops at the top and bottom of the ball to form crosses.

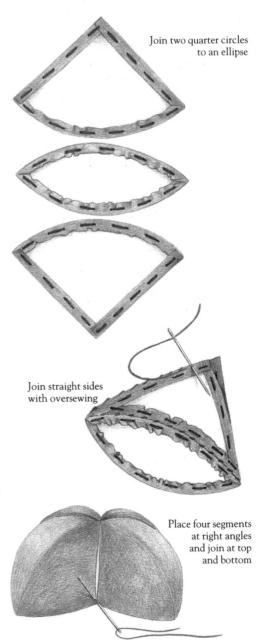

Join two quarter circles to an ellipse

Join straight sides with oversewing

Place four segments at right angles and join at top and bottom

Join the four centre
segments together

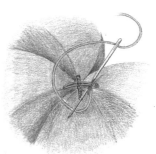

Work two buttonhole loops
to form a cross

Five little fishes

Use patchwork three-dimensionally to make a sparkling mobile for a shady corner. The double-sided patches are sewn together with the backing paper inside to give it body. Add colourful trimmings to complete the exotic fish.

Materials

Metallic fabric, 10×12in (25×30cm)
5 small bells
5 tassels
Felt pieces in orange, turquoise, yellow and
    green
Glue
Thread for tying
Flexible turquoise-coloured card
    $1^1/_2 \times 23^1/_2$in (4×60cm)

Preparation

1 Trace the diamond shape on page 10 and
transfer to card. Use the template to cut 10
papers.

2 Using the same template, cut 10 fabric
diamonds, adding $^1/_4$in (6mm) all round.

3 Pin a paper centrally to the wrong side of
each fabric diamond. Fold over edges and
baste (refer to page 45).

Making the fish

4 Place two diamonds with wrong sides
together and oversew around the edges.

5 Sew a tassel to each bell and stitch in
place to the bottom of each fish. Trace the
shapes on this page for the eyes and tail. Use
the patterns to cut felt eyes and tails. Glue
in position.

Finishing

6 Lay the card strip flat. Cut five threads to
8, 10, 12, 14 and 16in (20, 25, 30, 35 and
40cm) lengths. Neatly sew one end to each
fish, then glue or sew the other end to the
card, spacing them equidistantly.

7 Tape the card into a circle. Tie four
threads to the ring to hang the mobile.

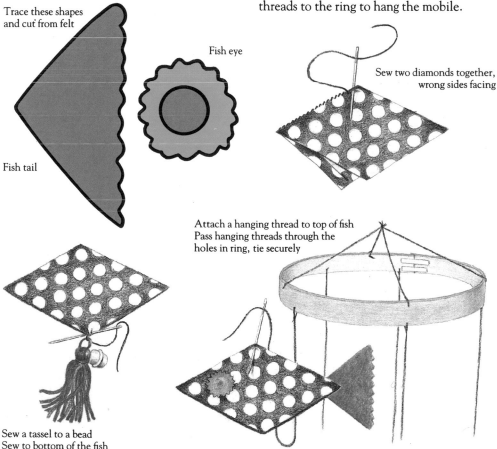

Trace these shapes
and cut from felt

Fish eye

Fish tail

Sew two diamonds together,
wrong sides facing

Attach a hanging thread to top of fish
Pass hanging threads through the
holes in ring, tie securely

Sew a tassel to a bead
Sew to bottom of the fish

4: IN STYLE

Lazy log cabin

Add some country style to a plain shirt with patchwork squares based on the Log cabin design. Instead of the traditional light and dark arrangement, the colours here are randomly arranged using a selection of pretty mini-prints.

Materials
Cotton fabric in eight different designs,
  10in × 36in (25 × 90cm) of each
Cotton backing fabric, 1yd (90cm) × 36in
  (90cm)
Chambray or cotton shirt

Preparation
1 Follow the instructions on page 42 to make Log cabin blocks, but work 4 rounds round the central 'chimney' square instead of three. Make 24 Log cabin blocks.

2 Join blocks in vertical strips of three, taking ¹/₄in (6mm) seams. Join strips together in pairs for fronts, matching seams. Join four strips together for back.

Finishing
3 Turn under ¹/₄in (6mm) along raw edges. Pin the patchwork blocks to the shirt, beginning at the button borders and working out to the sides.

4 Fill any spaces at the sides of the shirt by cutting strips of fabric to fit the patchwork and adding these to the block edges.

5 Using tiny hemming stitches, sew the top edges and the sides of patchwork to the shirt.

6 To neaten the lower edge, which may be shaped on some shirts, trim the shirt hem level with the patchwork. Turn under ¹/₄in (6mm) on patchwork and shirt and slipstitch the edges together.

7 Trim the inside of the collar stand with a strip of fabric.

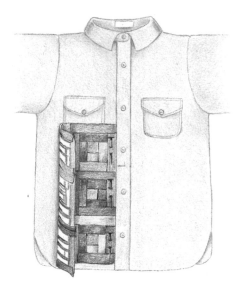

Pin patchwork to shirt, beginning at the button borders

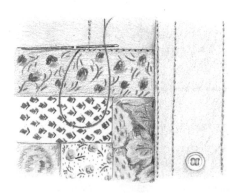

Attach blocks to shirt with hemming stitches

Magic carpet

Transform a colourful rug into a magic carpet bag with the art of strip patchwork. A fine, machine-woven rug is cut into strips then joined with spicy-coloured velvet patches to give the bag flexibility.

Materials
Small machine-woven rug
Oddments of velvet and velvet ribbon
Lining fabric, 1yd (90cm) square
Dressing gown cord, 1yd (90cm) long
9 eyelet fastenings, ¹/₂in (12mm) diameter
Cardboard
Strong, clear, quick-drying glue

Carpet thread
Double-pointed upholstery needle

Preparation
Note: When cutting both the carpet and velvet, be quite generous with the seam allowances as the two piles tend to work against each other under the machine foot.

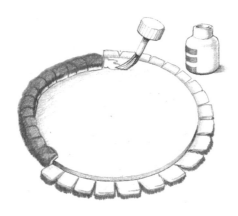

Snip into carpet circle edges, glue on to card circle

Sew the base into the bag using an upholstery needle

Insert eyelets 2in (5cm) below top edge of bag

1 Select detailed areas of the carpet and cut into strips and rectangles of at least 4³/₄in (12cm) wide, by any length. This is to allow for trimming and a ¹/₂in (12mm) seam.

2 Cut ten strips of carpet, velvet and velvet ribbon 22in (56cm) long and to any width.

Making the bag

3 Make up blocks of the 4³/₄in (12cm) wide strips to 19¹/₂in (50cm) deep. After stitching, trim the width of the blocks to 4in (10cm).

4 Lay the strips and blocks on a flat surface to make a pleasing arrangement of colours and shapes. Pin, baste and stitch seams. Trim the patchwork to an overall size of 19¹/₂ × 33in (50 × 84cm).

5 With right sides together, fold the edges of the patchwork to form a tube and stitch together.

6 Cut the lining fabric to the same dimensions as the bag i.e. 19¹/₂ × 33in (50 × 84cm), and with right sides together, stitch to form a tube.

7 With right sides facing, place the lining inside the carpet tube and stitch around the top edge.

8 Turn the bag right side out. Turn under the lower edge of the lining and patchwork and oversew together using carpet thread.

9 Cut a circle each of carpet and lining, 11¹/₂in (29cm) diameter. Cut two 9¹/₂in (24cm)-diameter card circles. Glue a cardboard circle to the wrong side of the carpet, folding over the edges. Repeat with the other cardboard circle and the lining fabric.

10 Working from the right side, thread the needle with carpet thread and taking one stitch through the cardboard circle and then one stitch from the bag tube, work all round the base. You may find it necessary to slightly ease the tube on to the base, taking smaller stitches from the base and larger ones from the tube to compensate.

Finishing

11 Insert the eyelets, 2in (5cm) below the top edge and evenly spaced around the bag. Thread the cord through the eyelets. Slip the lined base circle inside the bag.

81

One-off jewellery

Have you ever thought of patchwork jewellery? Single patchwork shapes make unusual and attractive earrings and a variety of templates is given on page 11 for you to use.

CHEQUERS

Materials
A pair of silver earring wires
2 rhomboid-shaped silver beads
Pieces of fancy and plain fabrics

To make earrings
1 Trace the square template from page 11 and use it to cut four papers and four fabric squares, two plain and two fancy.

2 Pin the papers in the centre of the fabrics, fold over the edges and baste.

3 Leaving the papers in place, baste and oversew one plain and one fancy square together.

4 Attach a bead and earring wire by securing a double thread to one corner of the earring, passing it up through the bead, looping into the earring wire then threading back down the bead to secure again with a stitch. Remove basting stitches.

TAKE THREE

Materials
Pieces of plain and fancy fabrics

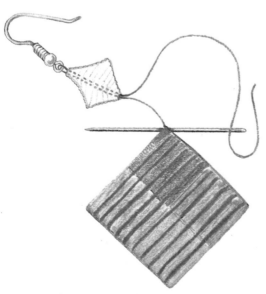

Secure thread to earring, thread through bead and earring wire, then back to earring

2 silver rose beads
2 silver shaped spacers
A pair of silver earring wires

To make earrings
1 Choose one of the triangular shapes on page 11 and cut out a template from card. Then cut 4 fabric triangles, two plain and two fancy, adding 1/4in (6mm) all round. Cut four papers using the same template.

2–4 Follow the instructions for the Chequers earrings, threading a spacer between the bead and earring wire in step 4

SIXTH SENSE

Materials
Pieces of fancy fabrics
2 beads
2 spacers
A pair of earring wires

To make earrings
1 Choose a hexagon shape from the template patterns on page 11. Cut four fabric patches, adding 1/4in (6mm) all round. Cut four papers, using the same template.

2–4 Follow the instructions for Chequers earrings.

Make a 'soft' jewellery pendant, using hexagons. Cut shapes from Lurex fabrics (mount thin fabrics on iron-on interfacing first) and sew together. Leave papers in position. Sew on glittering glass beads. Cut and sew on a fabric backing. Sew on a ring for hanging the pendant on a chain.

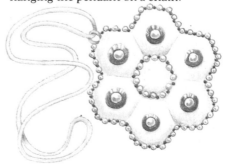

Clamshell collar

Inspired by the clamshell shape within a Liberty print, this Peter Pan collar has been transformed with pretty patchwork. Add a matching trim to a pocket top to complete this exquisite girl's blouse.

Materials
Pieces of white and patterned cotton fabric
Ready-made blouse

Preparation
1 Trace the clamshells on page 10 and transfer to cardboard. Use the templates to cut eight medium and 10 small papers. Cut eight medium clamshells in patterned fabric and 10 small clamshells in white fabric, adding ¼in (6mm) seam allowance all round. Position the clamshell template on the patterned fabric carefully to make the most of the print design.

2 Pin the papers to the fabric patches and fold over the curved edge, gathering a little and basting to secure. Keep the patch as flat as possible.

3 For the smaller patches only, fold the fabric on to the paper all round the patch.

4 Beginning at the collar front, position the patterned clamshells around the collar edge. If extra patches are required, add them to the back, overlapping from the sides.

5 Using tiny hemming stitches, secure the patches along the curved edges. Remove the papers.

6 Position the white clamshells around the collar, placing them in the semi-circles formed by the first row and overlapping by ¼in (6mm).

7 Turn under the points of the patterned clamshells so that they do not show, then stitch the white clamshells in place, removing the papers on the last edge. Work the pocket in the same way.

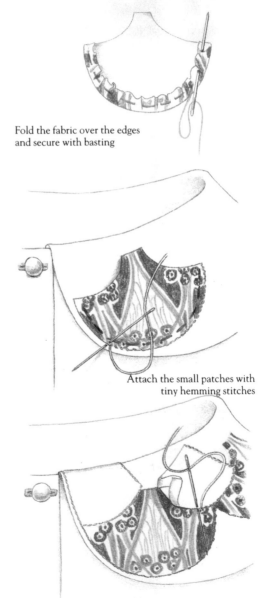

Fold the fabric over the edges and secure with basting

Attach the small patches with tiny hemming stitches

Overlap the patches by ¼in (6mm) and sew

Crazy notions

Crazy patchwork is closer in technique to appliqué than true patchwork. Born from the necessity to conserve fabric, crazy patchwork was transformed into an art form by Victorian needlewomen, who loved working with vibrant colours and luxurious fabrics.

Materials
Commercial waistcoat pattern
Pieces of velvet fabric of similar weight
Cotton fabric (for backing patchwork), ¹/₂yd (50cm)
Lining fabric for waistcoat back and lining
Lightweight wadding, ¹/₂yd (50cm)
5 ribbon roses
Embroidery silks in green, orange, rust, pink and red
Tiny beads

Preparation
1 Using the waistcoat pattern, cut out two waistcoat fronts from cotton fabric and lay on a flat surface.

2 Start at one corner by basting down the first patch. Then build up the patchwork by slipping new patches underneath the edges and securing in place with running stitches.

3 When the waistcoat fronts are completely covered with crazy patchwork, work over the raw edges of patches in herringbone stitch using embroidery silks.

4 Decorate the patches with embroidered flowers and butterflies using chain stitch and bullion knots. Add beads and ribbon roses for a touch of romance.

Finishing
5 When the patchwork decoration is complete, continue to make up the waistcoat following the pattern instructions. Cut a wadding interlining for the waistcoat back and baste to the lining before making up. This will give the back of the waistcoat some weight, to balance the patchworked fronts.

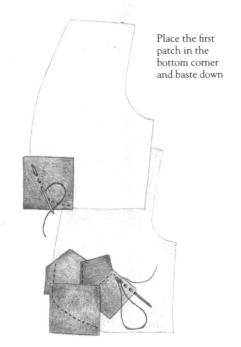

Place the first patch in the bottom corner and baste down

Slip patches under the edges of the first patch, secure with running stitches

Work herringbone stitches over the raw edges using different colours of silk embroidery thread

Baste wadding to the waistcoat back

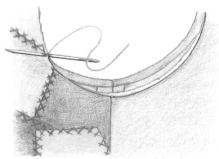

Catch the patchwork to lining with oversewing

American patchwork

Early American settler women had little beauty or luxury in their lives but, despite this they managed to create a kind of needlework that has developed into an art form.

The American tradition of patchwork began when early colonists from England and the Netherlands arrived in the east coast of America with the famous *Mayflower*. When the American weaving industry was in its infancy, most fabric had to be imported from England, therefore making all fabric an expensive and extremely precious commodity.

Every scrap of fabric was saved to economise and make new from old. Good pieces of fabric were salvaged from tattered clothing to use again and even those pieces which were discarded were re-cycled into padding for quilts. Salvaged pieces together with new off-cuts from dressmaking and tailoring went into the family 'rag-bag' which became a veritable treasure trove for patchwork.

Small geometric shapes were the basis of early patchwork pieces. Triangles, diamonds, rectangles and squares were cut out using templates to draw the shape and, like the artist's palette of colours, the patchworker built up a collection of coloured fabric shapes, designing each piece with instinctive colour co-ordination.

Quilts

The early American patchwork technique was most used for the design of quilts, although cushion covers, tea and coffee-pot cosies and curtains were also made. By the nineteenth century, patchwork was a national obsession. Patchwork quilts were essential additions to a bride's trousseau. They were also given as expressions of friendship, gratitude or sympathy and as prizes at local fairs. There were competitions for the best quilts and, as quilts became a part of society, the patterns and designs

came to reflect different aspects of life.

In the twentieth century new designs were passed on through national magazines and

newspapers as well as the traditional quilting bee meetings, where friends and neighbours gathered to construct a quilt. The quilting bee was a popular social event and important for passing on traditions. With the support of the quilting bee one person's two-month project could be completed in a day and rounded off with a party.

Designs

Everyday events and important occasions were represented by simple geometric designs. An arrangement of triangles could be instantly recognised all over the country as an abstract design for 'flying geese', a regular sight over New England.

Design templates were usually homemade and cut from wood, tin or cardboard to make the patches accurate and regular. As patchwork became more opulent and admired more for its artistic merit than for its functional nature, the templates became more expensive, being made from materials such as copper, brass and silver.

Traditional patchwork using mixed fabrics

Pieced patchwork

This type of patchwork used to be worked by hand, using running stitches. Nowadays, machine-stitching is often used, as it is quicker and longer lasting. Piecing is usually used for large quilts, made up of blocks, using squares, rectangles and triangles. Here are some traditional block patterns that have been popular for more than 200 years.

A treasury of history is contained in the names given to patchwork designs and many of them reflect the countryside observed by the settler women, religious symbols or occurrences in their daily lives. The designs are made in blocks which are then joined directly together or interspaced with strips of fabric or patchwork.

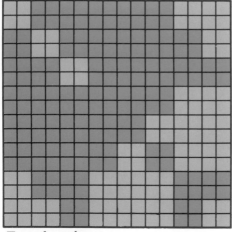

Tree of paradise

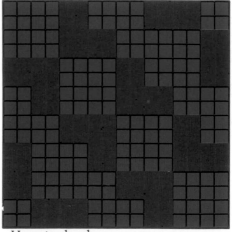

Hovering hawks

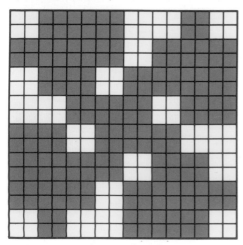

Chinese ten-thousand perfections

Iris

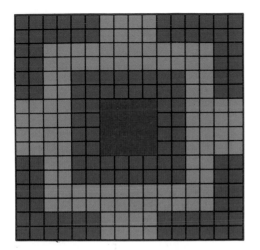

Tic-tac-toe

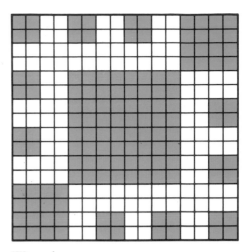

Winged square

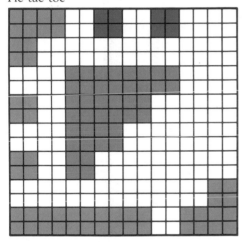

Fruit basket

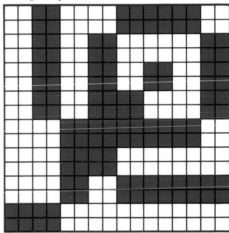

Love apple

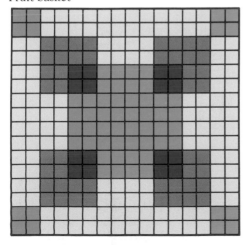

Rose garden

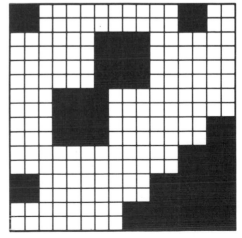

King's Crown

91

Peaches and cream

This duvet quilt design is one of the many traditional pieced patchwork designs that originate from America.

Materials

For a double size quilt 78in (1.95m) square:

Washable cotton/polyester fabrics in various colours

Cotton/polyester backing fabric, 84 × 92in (213 × 230cm)

Stiff cardboard

6 press fasteners

Preparation

1 Trace the shapes on page 95 and cut out templates A, B, C, D and F from stiff cardboard.

Place the card template on the wrong side of fabric and pencil round

Cut out the shape ¹/₄in (6mm) from the pencilled line

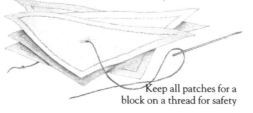

Keep all patches for a block on a thread for safety

2 Iron all fabrics smooth. Place a template on the wrong side of fabric and pencil round the shape carefully. Cut out ¹/₄in (6mm) from the pencilled line.

3 For each of the 25 complete blocks you will need one A square, four B squares, eight C triangles and four D triangles. The blocks are joined together with four E strips, measuring $10^5/_8 \times 1^7/_8$in (26.5×4.7cm), and four F squares.

4 For each of the 12 half-blocks (see diagram on page 94), cut one half A square, one complete and two half B squares, four C triangles and two D triangles.

5 For each of the four quarter-blocks, cut a quarter A, two half B squares, two C triangles and one D triangle.

Working the patchwork

6 Pin or baste the patches together, matching edges accurately. Work small running stitches along the pencilled lines, or use a medium-sized machine stitch. Secure the thread at the end of each seam. Take care in matching corners.

7 Join the patches together in strips first, then join the strips to the central A square to complete the block. Join completed blocks together with the E strips and F squares.

Peaches and cream
patchwork templates

Trace the shapes here and transfer to thick card. Cut out and use templates to cut fabric shapes.

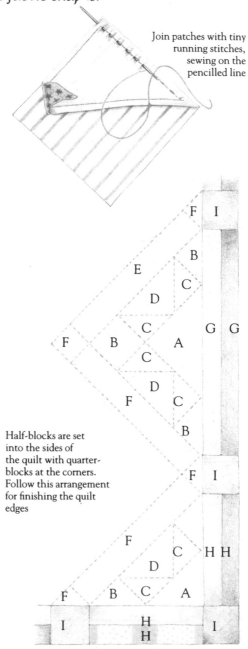

Join patches with tiny running stitches, sewing on the pencilled line

8 Make up the half-blocks and quarter-blocks. Sew them in place at corners and along edges.

Finishing
9 For the quilt border cut out 24 G strips $2^1/_2 \times 16$in (6×41cm), 16 H strips $2^1/_2 \times 8^1/_4$in (6×21cm) and 20 I rectangles $3^1/_2 \times 4^1/_4$in (9×11cm). Join strips and rectangles as the diagram.

10 Following the picture, stitch the borders to the quilt.

11 Cut the backing fabric to the same size as the patchwork. Also cut two strips of backing fabric 4in (10cm) wide by the width of the patchwork. Neaten one long edge of each strip.

12 With right sides together and raw edges level, sew the strips to the top edge of the patchwork and the backing fabric to form the quilt opening. Press strips to the wrong side.

13 Sew patchwork and backing fabric together using French seams. Sew the press fasteners evenly along the quilt opening.

Half-blocks are set into the sides of the quilt with quarter-blocks at the corners. Follow this arrangement for finishing the quilt edges

The Star quilt is, in fact, a duvet cover but could be made as a proper quilt. Baste wadding to wrong side of patchwork, spread lining on top. Stitch all round, bind the edges.
Ribbon quilting
Narrow ribbons make a pretty effect when used for tying quilts. Thread into a long needle. Take through the quilt from the top, bring through again to right side and tie tight knots.

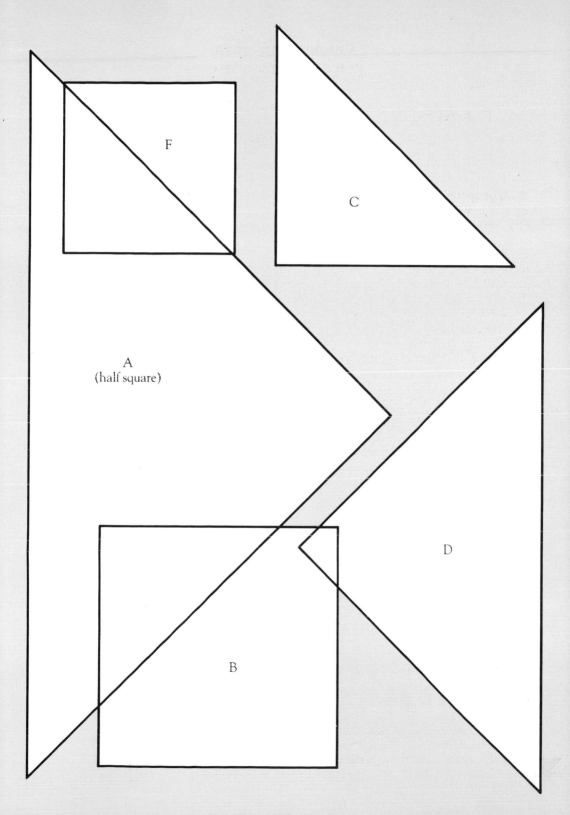

F

C

A
(half square)

D

B

Acknowledgements

All designs by Lynette Mostaghimi except: pages 16–17, 18–19, placemats and tablecloth by Anne Wilkinson; pages 20–21, 24–25, Somerset cushion cover and teacosy by Betty Fanning; pages 48–49, overnight bag by Anne Wilkinson; pages 54–55, children's quilt, pictures by Lucy Bower, sewing by Pauline Cohen; pages 66–67, child's duvet cover by Sylvie Mettyear; pages 70–71, Scottie dog by Pam Dancy; pages 94–95, pieced quilt by Cheryl Owen. The designs on pages 42–43 (pincushion), 56–57 (teddy bear) and 72–73 (baby ball) are from the Patchwork Dog and Calico Cat, Chalk Farm Road, London NW1. Special fabrics were kindly provided by The Quilt Room, 20 West Street, Dorking, Surrey. All ribbons by Offray Ribbons Ltd.